Toddler Discipline Guide

How to Discipline a Toddler without Yelling

Jordan Waldrop

Copyright © 2019 Jordan Waldrop

All rights reserved.

ISBN-13: 978-1-0831-4119-4

© COPYRIGHT 2019 BY **JORDAN WALDROP** - ALL RIGHTS RESERVED.

The content contained within this book may not be reproduced, duplicated or transmitted without direct written permission from the author or the publisher.

Under no circumstances will any blame or legal responsibility be held against the publisher, or author, for any damages, reparation, or monetary loss due to the information contained within this book. Either directly or indirectly.

Legal Notice:
This book is copyright protected. This book is only for personal use. You cannot amend, distribute, sell, use, quote or paraphrase any part, or the content within this book, without the consent of the author or publisher.

Disclaimer Notice:
Please note the information contained within this document is for educational and entertainment purposes only. All effort has been executed to present accurate, up to date, and reliable, complete information. No warranties of any kind are declared or implied. Readers acknowledge that the author is not engaging in the rendering of legal, financial, medical or professional advice. The content within this book has been derived from various sources. Please consult a licensed professional before attempting any techniques outlined in this book.

By reading this book, the reader agrees that under no circumstances is the author responsible for any losses, direct or indirect, which are incurred as a result of the use of information contained within this document, including, but not limited to, — errors, omissions, or inaccuracies.

CONTENTS

	Introduction	1
1	Understanding Life from a Toddler's Point of View	3
2	Love and Logic	7
3	Positive Praise	10
4	Causes and Effect	13
5	Rules and Rewards	16
6	Say What You Mean, Mean What You Say	20
7	Mommy's Helper	24
8	Know Your Triggers	27
9	Time for Yourself	31
	Conclusion	34

INTRODUCTION

When I was younger, my brother had an unexpected baby. My parents, of course, were elated but my brother and me? It's safe to say that we were both mortified. For him, it was because of the plummet his finances were going to take. For me, it was because my sister-in-law and I had never really seen eye-to-eye where disciplining children came into play.

She didn't believe in discipline. Her parents never disciplined her and therefore she saw no need to enforce discipline in her home. I had mentioned the lack of discipline was what caused her to be the way that she was. She wasn't impressed.

I was fearing for my little niece or nephew. I was afraid that I wasn't going to love him or her because it was going to be a little brat. Now listen, I have no problems with a naughty child. I used to lock my mother out of the house so I could get to the candy jar and eat in peace.

A child is supposed to be naughty. It's supposed to be a child, to test its boundaries. No child is perfect and it's not your job as a parent to raise them perfectly, but it is your job to teach them manners. It's your job to discipline them when they are being unruly. But you don't have to smack the child or yell at them to get your point across.

My mother never smacked my brother or me, although I still tell her that she had to give me more hidings because I got away with too much. She threatened us with her slipper, yes, but nothing to cause nightmares. My point is that you don't have to haunt your child's dreams with your discipline, but you do have to discipline them.

My sister-in-law's sister has a child. That child that opens every drawer, takes off every book from the bookshelf and dog-ears every page, and manages to get red lipstick on the ceiling. No one wants him around and why? Because he was never disciplined. I don't think he has ever heard of the word "time-out." He's 10 years old now and still, he is a dreaded human being. Now the parents want to discipline him, but he has gotten away with being a brat all these years, so he's not going to learn some manners now.

Children must be disciplined from a very young age. They need to be taught the difference between right and wrong, between what is acceptable and what is not. There must be rules and if a child doesn't abide by them, it's time to enforce some of that discipline.

Now, my brother and I are very similar. We get along well and never fight, not even as children. The things we got into trouble for involved a lot of scheming and candy. Now that I think about it, we mostly got into trouble because of candy. My mother had a different method to disciplining us and, if I'm being perfectly honest, I think it's what made my brother and me tolerable humans.

I made it my life's mission to teach parents who have tried everything with their kids. I decided to target toddlers as that is where discipline needs to start. Not when the kid is already a child or pre-teen. To new parents and experienced parents, I am sure this book will be of great use.

1 UNDERSTANDING LIFE FROM A TODDLER'S POINT OF VIEW

Do you remember the imaginary friend you used to keep in your closet when you were a child? Do you remember the innocent outlook on the world? Do you remember how much fun it was playing in the mud? No? Well, maybe it's time you remember.

A toddler hardly ever does something knowing that it's wrong the first time. They have been in this world for far fewer years than we have and it's our job to teach them these things.

Learning by Example

I remember very little about my childhood but there is one incident that I remember as clearly as if it happened yesterday. I was small, no older than three. It's probably my first and earliest memory. I used to love playing in the mud. I always told my parents that I was baking mud biscuits. One day, after my parents told me specifically not to clean my toys in the sink as the mud was going to clog everything up, I went and emptied an entire bucket's worth of mug in the sink.

My mother was furious and sent me to my room which shouldn't have been as big a punishment as it felt like. When my father returned from work, I got into my closet and hid behind the spare blankets. I was terrified because I knew that I made a very big mistake. When my father walked into the room, his voice booming like thunder, I managed to scrape together enough courage to get out of the closet. My dad's mustache didn't curl with anger as I anticipated, and his voice was a lot softer when he saw a teary-eyed three-year-old stumble out of a closet.

After I recited my apology that I had been working on all day, he sat me down on my bed, threw his arm around my shoulder and told me something terrible he did as a kid. I can't quite remember how the story went but I know that it made me giggle. Then he told me that we all make mistakes, but we have to learn from it. It sounds like a terrible thing to say to a toddler. How on earth do they even understand that?

The truth is there are more things that tots understand than we think. Sure, I might not have understood it fully back then, but I never forgot it. And when I grew older and the lesson finally sunk in, I understood why my father did what he did.

If he started yelling at me, if he lifted a hand, I would have been too terrified to even understand a word he was saying, let alone make sense of it all. The thing is, we shouldn't discipline our kids with fear. My father took a step back, imagined himself in my shoes and handled it accordingly. When I became older, he told me about the beatings and punishments he got as a child. He told me that it never taught him the things that he needed to know. It merely taught him the things he knew his parents didn't like him doing.

Things need to be explained and made clear to toddlers. Looking at the world from their point of view will make this so much easier. Toddlers get engrossed in the present and don't think about the consequences. They live in the past and the present but rarely take the time to look at the future and what consequences their actions will bring them.

Here are a few tips to help see things from a toddler's point of view and why each tip is important:

Consider what works from their point of view

Toddlers whine, cry, and yell for attention. Why? Because it works for them. To them, it's what gets you to give them attention. They don't care whether it's good or bad. It gets you to stop what you are doing and take a minute to listen to them or pick them up. They are smarter than what we give them credit for. This is something that I will repeat multiple times because it's something we shouldn't forget.

Acknowledge what they are feeling

Talking about feelings can be tough as an adult but young children don't really care. They can't yet understand why they should share their feelings and why not, so they are in an oversharing stage of their life that doesn't seem to end for a very long time. At least, that's what it feels like.

It's good to talk about feelings with them and to acknowledge what they are feeling. "I understand that you are angry," or "I know that you don't want to stop playing with your dolls" are good examples. When anything or anyone goes against a tot's wishes it's as if the entire world is turned against them and that is when they start acting up.

Letting them know that you understand all this makes things a little easier for them. Try to relate to them as well. Try using words like "I don't want playtime to end either."

Limited speech

Try to turn the time back in your mind and remember the vocabulary you possessed at the age of your toddler. It's not very big, is it? Try thinking of it as an Italian trying to speak to a German. Both parties are going to get upset when they don't understand each other. A toddler wants you to read their mind and they need you to know exactly where their vocabulary ends and where you should start using your own initiative.

Try finding the hints your child drops when they don't understand you. They may tilt their head to one side or might furrow their brow. Try explaining something in a simpler way to them.

"I see this one way and no way else"

Toddlers have a way of keeping one view and one view only. Say they want a cookie and you are telling them that they are not getting it because it's bad for them. In their minds, they are convinced that they want the cookie and don't understand that it's bad for them. They are still learning that there are different sides to a story and not just theirs. Be patient and try to explain it to them to the best of your abilities.

Set an example

It's also important to lead by example. Toddlers take on a lot of traits, good and bad, from their parents. At this tender age, they are like a sponge and take in anything and everything they possibly can. Yelling and raging will teach your child that it is alright to do this. No one wants a screaming tot and I can promise you that is what's going to happen if you give him the tiniest inkling that it's okay to behave in such a manner.

Setting an example might not put you in their shoes, but it will give them some shoes to step into. Kids are easily manipulatable and can be influenced quite easily. They will adapt to their surroundings because it's part of their instincts and they do not understand the world in the same way as adults do. They will take on the personality of whatever they need to survive.

There is nothing a child idolizes more than their parents and what better examples to follow? There will be times when you feel like you want to strangle the kid but remember that you are an adult and you need to set the example. Also, if the child sees you acting that way when there is trouble, it will give them the idea that it is okay to act like that around other children as well.

Freeze, Fight, or Flight

When you are putting yourself in their shoes and thinking like they are thinking, how do you react to a raging parent? Freeze, fight, or flight? None of these are remotely the reaction you are looking for in a child. Either they freeze and they shut you out entirely, fight and make you even angrier because, let's face it, if you do it, they will want to do it too, or choose flight. No parent wants a child to run away from them and hide. It goes against every paternal instinct we have.

Tots mirror our actions and if we are handling it calmly, so will they. Most tots will stop what they are doing and listen. But remember, just because you are being calm about the situation does not mean you can't be strict or firm. Sometimes the tot will need a firm voice to slow them down or coax them out of their shell so they will listen.

2 LOVE AND LOGIC

Children, no matter their age, tend to test a parent's limits and see just how far they can push. From the time they learn how to speak they practice the art of negotiating and they become masters in no time.

Whether they are begging, pleading, crying, or making promises that they know they will never keep, they will try to get out of whatever you are telling them to do or not to do. They will try everything and when they see that none of their efforts have paid off, they will throw a temper tantrum. The one thing every parent dreads. If we are lucky it will happen at home but when you are in a store and your tot wants something that they cannot get, they will whip out the big guns and cause a scene.

It's easy to just give in and give your child what they want seeing as he is attracting more attention than necessary. It's tempting to back down let your tot win this round because maybe you didn't get enough sleep, or you still have a hundred things to do before lunch and this one is just making things more difficult. The truth is that you can do that. You can choose which battles to lose and which ones to challenge.

Choosing Your Battles

When they are lashing out it's a sign of them becoming independent. They might be acting like complete brats but it's important to remember that you are encouraging them to make their own decisions and choices. In some cases, it is important for you to just give up a fight and let them win. This is not always the case and you certainly should not do it most of the time, but how do you expect your child to make their own decisions when you are taking over and winning every battle? If they know that they are fighting a losing battle every time, they will stop having a mind of their own entirely.

There are fights, however, that backing down and letting your child have their way simply won't do. You need to figure out which battles are fight-worthy and which ones are not. If you let your youngling have a small victory, they will be more content to let you have a bigger one because they do not understand that some things are more important than others.

Toddlers will go through stages and unlike grown-ups, their stages don't last very long. They will fight you for something longer than they will have use of that something.

For example, my eldest had fought me with all his might to wear his batman cape into town and to church. Being a new parent and wanting my child to be perfect, I refused outright and forced him to wear what I gave him. One day, when I was feeling particularly weary while tying his shoelaces, he asked me to wear his cape once again.

I was in no mood for a quarrel and I had enough on my plate that day. I knew that he was only going to his grandmother's house so there was no harm in it. So, I strapped him into the car-seat without even the smallest of hassles and had a quiet drive. He did have an annoying, gloating look on his face but it was tolerable because he was quiet, and I wasn't having an argument with a three-year-old.

My mother gave me a knowing look when we arrived and she said "ah, so you've finally learned which battles to fight," and I was shocked. She knew from the start and she said nothing to help me. I was angry but then I realized that she was never going to get through to me anyway. My skull was too thick, and I wanted a perfectly dressed child without a Batman cape.

When we got back home, the cape was discarded in the living room and he never looked at the thing again. He had his few hours of victory and he was perfectly content. We had been fighting over that cape for over a week and it took mere hours for him to gloat and give it up forever.

I did not carry on making the mistake of fighting useless battles anymore and I started to use it to my advantage. Whenever two arguments were going on, one about a crown and one about taking medicine, I used it to my advantage. "Yes, you can wear the crown, but you have to take your meds first." Instantly, content with the battle they have won, they relent.

Things concerning their health and safety are not negotiable, and you will do anything and everything to get the child to take their medicine. But there might be ways that you can use another argument to get what you want. The tot won't know the difference because they got something that they wanted. You will be distracting and redirecting everything and still get done what needs to get done. Even if it requires a little bit of sacrifice on your end. Your tot will be sacrificing as well without even knowing it.

So, choose your battles wisely and always have something up your sleeve. Just because you are waving a white flag does not mean that you have lost. You are merely distracting your tot from the real issues at hand and redirecting their focus. If they have something new to fight over and win, they will forget about the other fight going on.

Most of the time they fight just because they are stubborn and that's just the way it is—you did nothing wrong as a parent. It's just your time to use your years and knowledge as an advantage to give you and your child what both of you want and have some peace and quiet in the meantime. Fighting over trivial things is not as important as keeping a bond with your child. Choosing your battles is a great way of keeping that bond.

3 POSITIVE PRAISE

Let me ask you this...

When you are at work and your boss comes around, sees the stack of documents you have already processed and praises you, what do you feel? It feels good, doesn't it? It makes you want to take on more work. It's nice to know someone sees the effort you are putting in. It's nice to know that someone has acknowledged your good work.

Well, I have news for you. It's a tactic to get you to work harder. Sure, they did see that you are working harder than any other employee or else they wouldn't have noticed your work, but they don't have to praise you. What you are doing is in your job description. It's what's expected of you. But when you are praised it makes things so much better. It gives you something to brag to your colleagues about or even your significant other.

We as human beings crave the acceptance of others no matter how hard we try to tell ourselves otherwise. We like it, we want to bathe in all the good things that get said to us, the compliments and praises. It comes as no surprise that it is a well-known tactic to get employees to pull more than their weight. If it works, it works. But why not implement that same strategy with your tot?

Praising Your Toddler

Toddlers love praise and they love being told they are being good. Our younglings have more instincts in these matters than grown-ups do. The heartaches of life haven't stripped away their natural instincts yet.

As I have mentioned before, it's only natural for people to crave the approval of others. Your tot looks up to you and will look up to you for the rest of their life. Getting your approval is a big thing for them. If they know that they are going to get it when they are good, why would they be bad?

Most children, not all, misbehave because there's a lack of praise. They misbehave to get your attention. It's the only way they know how to.

By using praise, you are telling your kid what you want them to do and what you do not like them doing. It gives them a reason to behave because when they are getting your attention when they are not being bad, why would they want to be bad?

Praise is also a great way to build up your child's self-esteem from a young age and teach them how to think positively about themselves and their actions. It tells your youngling what they are doing is good and they deserve the praise that they are getting.

When a child is always getting scolded there's a good chance that they will doubt everything they do in the future. They won't strive to do good things because all they have known to get is lectures and disapproval anyway. Therefore, most kids act up.

We show disapproval without even knowing it. Simple things like "you put the toys in the wrong box" can make your child wonder whether they will ever do the right thing. In their little minds, this activity is associated with disapproval and they won't do it again. They don't understand it is the wrong box. They only understand it is a box. Replace your phrase with "thank you for putting your toys away. You're so good at this, why don't you try putting it in that box next time." This will make your tot see that "wow, mommy/daddy approves" and will try their best to keep it that way.

Praise can be used for many things, like putting away toys or putting down the doll when it's time to get dressed. It may get tedious sometimes, but it works. Your child will learn exactly when praise is given and how to get it. They're smart like that.

Creating Choices

It seems odd to give a toddler a choice, doesn't it? The truth is this gives them a sense of power and control. As with grown-ups, toddlers like to have a say in the things they do. It will teach them how to make good choices and deal with the consequences of bad ones. Some children don't mind not having choices and will literally go along with everything you say and tell them to do. Where other younglings will lash out and get frustrated.

If you are making the choices for them, you are influencing the person they are on their way of becoming. A person needs to make choices to guide their lives in a certain direction and, despite what many parents might believe, their choices are not always the best for their children. Not to mention the effect it will on them as they grow up. Indecisiveness is mostly caused by a lack of freedom in choices as children. When you don't have to make choices, how will you react when you do need to make choices? It will cause you to doubt yourself and the choice you are about to make.

I am one of those people. I can't make a choice to save my own life but it's not from lack of trying from my parents. They encouraged me from a young age to make decisions. Some people are just wired differently. Still, it's a parent's responsibility to do everything in their power to encourage the ability of their child to make their own decisions, even if one day they will still be faced with indecisiveness. It will also help you along the line of parenting. No one wants to baby a child until they get married, so teaching them from a young age how to make good decisions will help you avoid those instances as much as possible.

A good thing to do is to decide on easy choices that won't affect things too much, such as asking your tot what story they would like to hear or whether they would like to play with dolls or do crafts today.

Make sure that you give your tot choices where you can agree to any decision they make. If you ask them whether they want to do crafts that day, but you can't, don't be surprised when your youngling has a full-on tantrum. Rather, replace crafts with something they can do on their own if you are unable to sit with and monitor them. Don't ask things like "do you want to take a nap?" because the answer will be "no" most of the time. If you force the kid to take a nap, they will feel like they had no choice even when you asked them, and they will avoid making choices in the future.

It is a great way of teaching your child discipline. When your toddler is acting up, take the choices away. Let them know exactly what they did wrong and why you are doing this. It's an effective punishment for any child. Don't forget to praise your child when they are making decisions!

Releasing Control

This is a hard one for any parent to see through. You must accept that there are certain things you cannot control. And there are even more things that can go other ways than your own.

When you are keeping a tight leash on your child it's easy for them to act up and feel trapped. By giving your child a choice, you are giving up some form of control, but you are also making your life a lot easier. Children tend to behave better when they believe that they have a choice in the matter.

No one likes to be controlled and some toddlers show signs of this at a very young age. Better to give up that tiny piece of control than to struggle with an unruly child for years to come.

4 CAUSES AND EFFECT

Not many people realize that there is a difference between punishment and consequences. I never knew the difference before I dove in a little deeper and did some more research. A consequence is the result of something that someone did whereas punishment is to cause someone to suffer. It's sometimes hard to deliver the consequence but these following two tips will help you with just that.

There's Always a Consequence

Act, don't talk
"If you do not stop throwing your peas on the floor, you are not getting dessert." Isn't that a simple consequence we always try? The fact is, your tot will not believe you. They live in the "now" and do not think that they won't get dessert. Warn them but don't mention it again and when it's time for dessert, tell your tot that you warned them and because they threw their peas on the floor, they are not getting any dessert. When they see that you are serious about things like this, it will stay in their memory. Throwing their peas on the floor will be associated with no dessert. They will think twice before they do it again.

Don't cave
A mistake I frequently see is parents caving in. When the tot is starting to cry because they did not get dessert, they will cave with an "I will give it to you now, but next time you will not get." The memory that they can cry to soften your heart will be planted in their head and they will use it with anything you take away or make them do as a consequence. They had the choice between throwing their peas on the floor or having dessert. They chose the peas which means they are not getting dessert. It's hard to look at

your youngling's face in situations like these but it's important to pull through.

Now, you might wonder what some relatively good consequences might be but don't fret, my friend, I've got you covered.

Time out
Choose a place that your child will associate with negative consequences. It has to be well away from any distractions or toys. Don't put them in their room or in their crib. You want them to have only positive feelings toward those places. Not to mention that their room is filled with toys and that is hardly a time out.

A time out is supposed to allow your child to cool down and think about what they have done and the consequences that follow. Keep them in full view and make sure that they are not misbehaving by running around or sneaking toys.

The bickering table
Sometimes the dinner table can feel like this. Always bickering, jabbing, and arguing—mostly the children who have beef with each other. This isn't as much a consequence as resolving the problem at hand. If you have more than one child who enjoys pestering each other, sit them down at the table and let them bicker it out. They will grow tired of it sooner or later. Instead of telling them to stop again and again, let them sort it out themselves.

Take a privilege away
This can be anything from arts and crafts to music or videos on the iPad. Those things are all privileges and trust me if those things are taken away, your tot will notice it. When they ask for it, simply reply with "no, I told you not to pull the cat's tail, but you went and did it anyway. Now you are not getting your videos."

Use "the phrase"
Remember when you were a kid and your mother used to say to you "You can only come inside when your feet are washed?" That is the phrase that is effective from the tot years to the teen years and can be adjusted and tweaked for every age group. It's easy enough to perfect and it is very effective as well. "I'll know you're ready to play with your truck if you put away your Spiderman first, otherwise you keep playing with your Spiderman." Choice and consequence.

No books at bedtime

I refuse to do this because I think I enjoy bedtime stories more than the actual child. I love books, always have, and I have made it my life's mission to help my children adopt the love I have for them. However, I do have friends that say this works wonders. Whenever their kids are acting up before bed, they warn them about no bedtime stories and when they still go on, they get nothing. Only a kiss on the head and a "sleep tight." Apparently, it has only happened once and never again. Seems like it's a useful tip for the parent with a particularly naughty bedtime child.

No more playing

As a child, the worst thing that can happen is when playtime is being taken away or cut short. From toddlerhood to childhood, a kid's only goal is to play as much as they possibly can. When this privilege is being taken away because they are being difficult, it can be a very hard lesson learned for them and they will do anything to get it back. When they aren't playing, what else is there for them to do, anyway? Nothing will get your tot to get their act back together faster than playtime being taken away.

South African method

When I was in South Africa visiting a cousin, he told me a very interesting method his wife has. South Africa is still very fond of giving their children hidings and although it is frowned upon by a vast majority of the world, it seems to work for them.

Another way, the way that I want to mention, is something completely different though. I noticed his wife tell their kids that they must eat the food they don't like first and then they can move on to the other nice things. So, there I sat, watching as three little Afrikaans children ate their peas, then their cabbage, then their potato before moving to their meat and rice.

My cousin leaned over and told me that it was the only way they could get any of them to eat their vegetables. If they don't eat their veggies, they don't get the nice food. Then I looked over at my cousin's wife and there she was, eating her peas first, then her cabbage, then everything else. Get all the bad stuff done before doing the good stuff. Personally, I think this is a great thing to live by as an adult as well as a kid.

5 RULES AND REWARDS

On my fridge, I have a board that my kids helped make. On the board are three sections (the number of kids in the house) and in these sections stickers or magnets get stuck. It's high enough for them not to reach and cheat but still low enough for them to see.

These stickers go toward a specific reward. For example, we have dessert every night. Before you have a heart attack, it's only a cookie. Most of the time healthy, homemade ones. Five stickers mean that they get dessert that night. With every chore that is done and with every good deed, they get a sticker.

Establishing Rules for Your Toddler

For toddlers it's a little different because they can't grasp the concept until they are a little older, but we still work with a reward system even with the toddler. We have set rules like putting away toys before leaving a room or eating the food you don't like first. It's not easy to bring these rules into the house without a reward system in place.

Here is a list of rules and rewards we have set up for our own toddler that work:

Use your inside voice when you are inside the house

Don't you just hate it when you are having a nice afternoon with some friends and suddenly, the kids start yelling and laughing so loud that you can't hear each other when you speak? That is exactly what inside voices are for. As soon as a toddler starts screaming, I put them outside and sit with them. Whenever they want to go inside, I say, "not until you've learned to use your inside voice." It's an effective way to make any toddler, (and child) use their inside voices. Inside is where all the toys are, anyway.

Do not climb on the furniture

Once they can walk and talk, it's hard to get them to shut up and sit still. The talking I can still handle but the constant climbing? I am a nervous wreck. Not only because it is no place for a toddler to sit on a coffee table, but it's also very dangerous. Tables have sharp corners, chairs are high, and television cabinets contain things more expensive than the toddler's entire room. You don't want them to knock your television off the stand and you sure don't want them to knock the crystal vase from the coffee table. This is an essential rule that must be met with strict consequences.

Don't open drawers

When I was little, my mother's cousin used to visit with their little child. She was terrible and got away with murder. While my mother and her cousin used to talk, the kid would sneak around and go through everything my mother owned. Sometimes she returned to the conversation with things kids should never see. It got so bad that my mother told her cousin that she shouldn't visit anymore if she brought her child.

It was wrong to despise the child so much because her mother should have taught her better and whenever my mother mentioned something she'd reply with "children will be children." No, ma'am. Children will most definitely not go through a stranger's personal possessions just because their parents are too lazy to teach them any better. This is why this is such an important rule in my house.

Don't touch anything that doesn't belong to you

Toddlers break things. It's just the way it is. When there's a toddler in the house, it's best just to put away all the nice things and wait until they are older to take them out again. But when you visit someone else, you don't want your child's sticky hands on everything, not to mention the apologies you need to make when your child breaks something. Don't touch anything that isn't yours unless you have permission.

Don't leave a room without putting your toys away

Toddlers are messy and this carries on through their entire childhood. You have to teach them from a very young age that they need to put everything away before they leave a room to keep everything neat and tidy.

We never had this rule in the house as I was growing up and I feel for my poor mother. With my brother and me so similar in age, we had a ball with every single toy we owned, and I remember the mess that we made like it was yesterday. I vowed that I would never allow my own children to cause me that much of a hassle. It's not hard for them to put the toy away that they were playing with. It will teach them responsibility and give you fewer grey hairs to boot.

No fighting

In a house with three children and one toddler, it can sometimes get a little heated. No person is the same and when there is even the smallest of disagreements, the entire house explodes into chaos. This kid hits this one with a ball of socks, the other one slams his door shut, the toddler bites and screams at whoever gets in their way. It's like a movie but without the humor.

As parents, we get exasperated. This is when each of them must go downstairs and sit at the bickering table so they can fight to their heart's content. They also get no dessert for a few days. Why? Because they know that there are better ways to settle their differences than to fight. With the tot, it can be a little rough because they can't speak their minds properly yet, so we just put her in a time out after listening to her side of the story (which is usually just a load of babble and incoherent accusations), but it's important to let the toddler know that she is being listened to as well.

Rewarding Good Behavior

It's hard to come up with suitable rewards for your toddler. Some people go overboard with sweets and toys because they can't think about other rewards, they can give their kids. Here is an effective list of rewards that I have tried, tested, and improved to fit my tots and my pocket.

Here are some rewards I like to give my kids:

Movie of their choice

Who doesn't love a good movie on repeat? The answer is only a tot, but that's okay because at least they ate all their peas instead of tossing them at their brothers. You don't have to sit with the tot the entire time either, they get caught up in the movie and don't notice when you slip away to finish some chores in the kitchen. In general, when a tot wants to watch a movie that they have seen a hundred times, you will tell them no, but if you give it to them as a reward, you can't refuse to let them watch it.

A trip to the zoo/museum/park

Consider your budget when you are giving out this reward. I encourage children to be outside and to explore so a park is always a good idea. They might even make some new friends while they are there! A zoo and a museum allow your tots to learn new things and words while feeling like they are getting a reward.

An extra story before bed

Bedtime stories are sometimes too short, and your tot will be asking for "just one more" on more than one occasion. Toddlers love stories and when you do not usually cave and tell them another story, this is a good way to reward them.

A game
Whether it's a toddler's board game, a puzzle, or a video game, this will be a great reward for any tot. My partner and I are both big gamers and the tot wants to play along whenever we get our headsets out. Needless to say, whatever we are playing is not suitable for a toddler.

Here is where a game on the tablet comes in. They will feel like they are joining in on the fun while not influencing your high score in the slightest. It's both a reward and a way to keep them busy while you are getting some me-time.

A cookie
The simplest thing to do is to give your child a cookie as a reward but as much as they love that, their weight and health do not. Be careful what sort of treats you give your tot and make sure that they are healthy and good for them. I usually add fruit into the cookies because my tot absolutely detests the texture of the fruit.

6 SAY WHAT YOU MEAN, MEAN WHAT YOU SAY

It's important to say what you mean and stick to it. When someone tells you one thing and does the complete opposite, you will lose faith in that person because they were obviously lying. Children work with credibility and if they are misbehaving even after you've used the "I'm warning you, if you do that again, it's a time out," that means that you have no credibility in their eyes. Whether it's a teacher or a parent, credibility is very important to a tot's and a child's discipline.

Don't Back Down

Be consistent

Consistency is important to any form of parenting. Children are drawn to consistency because they feel as if they can predict the outcome. This makes the phrase "I'm warning you, if you do that again, it's a time out," hold more power because they know when you tell them it's going to happen, it will happen.

Even tots have the tendency to play two parents against each other and it can make for a lot of trouble, not only for the kid, but for your relationship. Consistency doesn't only reach you but has to reach your partner as well. The two of you need to settle on one way of handling things and sticking to it no matter what the child says. It will get hard and your child will push against the boundaries you have set, but the key is to keep things consistent and not giving your child any slack.

Once you start giving third and fourth chances, they will assume you will always give it and act out when you are going back to only giving them two chances. If your partner is feeling particularly tired, it's your job to pick up the slack and keep things consistent and vice versa. This will give the two of you more credibility in your tot's eyes and they will realize that they cannot get away with bad behavior even when they try to play the two of you against each other.

Go through with your threat

No one likes a person who's more bark than bite, and in this case constant barking will not get you anywhere anytime soon. If you are threatening your child with a time out or no dessert, go through with it. When you are constantly telling your child that you are going to do something and never end up doing it, they won't take the threat seriously and will go on with whatever shenanigans that caused you to threaten them in the first place. It might be hard to resist their doe eyes when they beg for a treat, but you have to stay strong. It's going to be better for both of you in the long run.

Keep your promises

Much like your threats, it's important to stick to your promises. When you promised your tot that you would be going to the zoo, keep it as best you can. If you promise them a treat for good behavior and you never give it to them, they won't see the use of being good because they are never getting anything in return anyway. Tots are smart and can put two and two together even if they don't realize it yet. It will also teach them that keeping promises is important and that they should never make promises that they know they can't keep. You must set an example while also disciplining and rewarding your tot. Being a good example becomes a full-time job when your child is born.

Don't be unreasonable

Remember that you are encouraging your tot to become their own person and arguing about things concerning them is one step toward that. You do not want a brainwashed child, only a well-behaved one.

They are under you care and under your roof and what you say goes. You are still giving them choices in other matters but when they aren't listening to the few things you are not giving them a choice in, then it's time to face the consequences.

Your tot is still learning which buttons to push and which decisions they get to make for themselves. Give them a chance or two and afterward when you see that they are not backing down, you can reprimand him.

Keep the consequences tame at first and when it becomes apparent that your tot is going to misbehave in the same way repeatedly, it's time to push it up a notch or two. Starting out with no dessert for a week is unreasonable, so start out with a short time out or no ice cream when you go to the park. You don't want to be the complete bad guy from the get-go.

Don't back down

When your toddler is arguing with you about a punishment or a reward— mine has the tendency to want to switch rewards for others—it's important not to back down and give them what they want. They need to learn that they cannot always get what they want. If they grow up with that illusion in their minds, then they will feel cheated once they go to school when they get older.

Teachers do not care as much as you do as a parent and will never give your child exactly what he or she wants. Teach them that they will not get what they want all the time and that they cannot argue or cry their way out of things. They will try it again and again but the more you stand your ground, the less they will do it. It will be hard at first, but you will reap the benefits soon enough.

When you have made a decision, stick to it. You are still the parent and you get the final say. You do give up some form of control every so often, but you are ultimately still the boss. Don't let your tot walk all over you. It's the making of a very ill-behaved child when they get older and realize the power that they actually hold in the house.

Remember that both you and your partner need to stand firm in this role, so the tot cannot play the two of you against each other. Once they realize that you two are disagreeing, they will do everything in their power to use it to their advantage. When a toddler wants something, there isn't much they won't do to get it. The only way to prevent this is by staying firm and not backing down. They will learn soon enough.

Keep it short and sweet

You don't have to over explain yourself, because the tot doesn't understand half of what you are saying anyway. Keep your explanations short and sweet and don't leave room for arguments. You know exactly what you have said, and you do not need your toddler to twist your words like they so love doing.

Keeping it short and sweet will give your tot the realization that what you said is final and there is nothing more to be said. Use words that you know your tot understands and keep your sentences short. Don't confuse them with more words than necessary.

Use different sentences

Toddlers can get bored when they hear the same thing over and over again. When you repeatedly tell them to "stop singing in the house!" they will start to ignore you. Perhaps they will even annoy you from the very first time you say it to them. Instead, try saying something else like "you know mommy loves your voice, but maybe you will sound even better when you go to your room and sing there." They do not understand that you won't hear them anymore and it will mean peace and quiet for you.

7 MOMMY'S HELPER

It's important to make your tot feel like they are a part of the family. It's easy to exclude them whenever the family is doing something. Chores, game night, movie night, you name it. They are always put to bed first, given attention separately, and the bigger kids don't like playing with them.

A Part of the Family

You have to remember and remind the rest of the family that the toddler is as much a part of the family as they are. The tot might be new and may not understand very much, but they can feel when they are being excluded.

If you have other kids, it is unfair to expect them to take care of the tot while they are doing the things they do. Teenagers don't want to manage a tot when they are hanging out with friends and children don't want tots to play with their toys. It's your job to involve them in the other things that you do as a family. They will lash out when they feel left out and, in their heads, they will feel abandoned.

Here are a few ways you can involve your tot without it having to be an effort:

Take them shopping

It's hard to go shopping with a toddler who has a lot of energy, and they do enjoy causing some mischief along the way. It's easy to just drop the tot off at grandma's house and do the shopping alone. But taking your tot shopping can be both fun and educational for them.

When your youngling is getting unruly, make a game out of it by telling them to look around and point at whatever has a red wrapper or maybe teach them some new words of the ingredients you are putting into the cart. Just be sure that your tot is not putting their own shopping into the cart with yours.

When doing chores, involve them

I quite like involving my tot when I am baking. I call her "my little helper" and her face just lights up. Whether I pick her up so she can stir the contents of the bowl or press the cookies flat with a hand, she will go around telling the entire house that she alone has done all the baking.

Involve them during game night

The tot doesn't have to understand Monopoly to play it with the family. Merely let them pick up a card or carry the money between one player and the other. Let them throw the dice or move the little statues. My tot has a thing for carrying the money around and asking for a hug or a kiss in return. You'd be surprised how much your tot will love being involved.

Everyone Has a Job to Do

It's important for your tot to understand that there is a job for everyone in the family and by having your youngling help you with chores and everyday tasks, it makes them realize that they must help around the house too. This will prepare them for chores when they are older.

Remember that you are never alone and that there are always other moms that struggle with the exact same issues that you do. Try looking for a community of toddler moms. Whether it's in your neighborhood or on social media, it helps to know that you are never alone.

There are things that you might think your toddler is doing that no other toddler has ever done and you might not know how to handle it. A community of parents with tots is a great way to ask for help and advice. Not to mention the rocking play dates that might come from it.

Friends are essential for your child to grow and learn how to communicate properly before school. When your tot is surrounded by well-behaved children, they will mimic their friend's actions. Toddlers are considered sheep in the sense that they always want to do what their friends are doing. Pick the right community for your tot to grow up in and maybe they can be an example for the other kids. It's rewarding to see your child be the leader and it warms your heart to see that they are making friends while you are making friends as well.

If there aren't communities like this in your area, why not go to the local park? It's a great way to get to know other mothers. Not all countries have safe parks to go to with children and that's a sad part of life but if you know that there is a place near you that is safe for both you and your tot, don't avoid it. You might meet some strange people, but you might meet some people who can help you raise your tot the best possible way that you can.

Communities are also great in the long run. When your tot makes a friend early on in life, they will have friends when they go to school or need to be socially active. Making friends can be hard but toddlers don't have the shyness of children, teens, or adults. They make friends much easier and chances are that they will stick around for a very long time because they already have a bond.

8 KNOW YOUR TRIGGERS

Screaming toddlers is one of the things that makes me want to run to the hills. I can't stand it. It's safe to say that it is my biggest parental flaw. I can't stand a naughty and misbehaving child. It drives me absolutely mad. I lose my temper very quickly and it's the worst thing you can possibly do. It happens, though, because we are all human. We are all just people trying to survive as best we can.

Life isn't easy and with a misbehaving tot, well, it makes everything harder than it needs to be. You will lose your temper and you will want to hand the child over to your significant other and run for your life. It's normal.

Steps to a Calmer You

A toddler is going to act up sooner or later and here are a few tips that I have learned to keep myself calm in these situations:

Take care of yourself

It's not easy, but it's a must-do when you are raising a kid. When you are stressed, overworked, hungry, or tired, dealing with things get hard. It makes a person fidgety and puts them on the edge. The tiniest inconvenience makes you lash out at the child and makes the situation so much worse. When your child is having a tantrum and you are yelling at them, they will try to yell louder than you and the cycle will go on. Keep yourself and your mind in a good and logical state so you can handle your child to the best of your abilities.

Stop and think

When your tot is on the floor, throwing their hands and legs around like a hooligan, stop what you are doing and think for a second. Is what you are about to do is going to make this any better or worse for you? Is the tot going to stop if you start yelling at them? Are they going to come over to you, hug you, and apologize?

If the answer is no, then it's best you not go through with it. Sometimes just stopping and looking at your child will cause him to stop completely. When I was a child and I had a tantrum, my mother would just cross her arms and look at me. She didn't say anything, didn't tap a foot or raise an eyebrow, she just looked at me. It made me so uncomfortable that I stopped what I was doing immediately. In some cases, it works on tots as well. It's definitely worth a try and if it doesn't help, at least it clears your head.

Ignore

I am one of those people who can't let things slide. I take one mean comment or one unnecessary remark and make an entire mountain from it. It's never effective and it never turns out in my favor and I have worked hard at ignoring things. It came in very handy with the kids.

Ignoring a child might seem mean but when it's their fourth tantrum about not getting cookies, it's safe to say that it's time to just ignore them. Pretend like you are not hearing them. Pretend that it's nothing to you and go on with whatever you are doing. Your ears might feel like they are bleeding and your hands might be twitching but as soon as a toddler sees that they are not getting the attention they are trying to get with the tantrum, they will stop and mope. Moping is much easier to deal with than a screaming child.

Breathe and take a time out

Take the time to stop and breathe whenever you feel like you are on the verge of lashing out at your tot. Take a deep breathe from your belly and close your eyes. Helping your body calm down naturally can do wonders.

Personally, whenever someone tells me to calm down and breathe, I want to hold my breath out of spite because there has never been a situation where telling someone to calm down and breathe has made them calm down and breathe. But knowing why this works may shed some light on why I am telling you this.

Your brain is telling your body that it is an emergency. Your brain is your own biggest enemy because it likes to overreact and cause you to make stupid decisions. When you are taking the time to breathe, you are reminding your body that it is not an emergency at all.

This is your kid, this is a little piece of you that you do not want to lash out at. Your brain can manipulate you into doing a lot of things, but you can also manipulate your brain. Be smart and remember that your child does not know this, and they do not understand that what they are feeling isn't worth the consequences. You still need to teach them that.

Instead of yelling, whisper

Yelling has never worked for whatever child I have taken care of or raised. Instead, I adopt a low, stern voice that they need to work for to hear. The calmer and gentler your tone is, the bigger the impact on your child will be. Children get on edge when you are getting angry and when you are speaking softly, they will feel more at ease and absorb what you are saying much easier—most of the time. Speaking softly will have your toddler stop what they are doing so they can listen.

The right sort of timing

It's easy to decide that it's time to discipline or teach your child a lesson as soon as they are acting up, but the truth is that you need to choose your timing very carefully. Teaching them a lesson when the situation has cooled down and you aren't ready to claw at the walls is the best time to do it. When a child is having a tantrum, they won't want to listen to you when you are trying to teach them something. Wait for your tot to calm down before bringing it up and telling them that it is not nice to throw a tantrum and ask them what they can do differently next time.

Stop it before it gets worse

If there is a chance that you can get your child to calm down before their tantrum, grab it with both hands. Tots are still new to the world and whenever something doesn't go according to plan, they lash out entirely. They don't know how to regulate their emotions which means that they don't know that they can handle things differently and more effectively.

When they are starting to feel lonely or hungry, take the time to comfort them or give them something to eat before it gets out of hand. There is no waiting for a tot, so whenever you think "I just want to finish this episode before I feed them" you will most definitely end up with an unhappy tot.

Lower your expectations

We all want the perfect, well-behaved child but the truth is that there will never be a perfect child. A child will lash out and test their limits, they will spit out their peas and rip the heads from their dolls. Lower your expectations. Instead of getting angry at the small things, sit them down and explain why what they are doing is wrong. There are far worse things they can do. Tots don't understand why they shouldn't do certain things and it's unreasonable to have high expectations for them.

Understand that you are not perfect

No parent is perfect, and you should never think that you are a failure as a parent whenever your youngling lashes out. They will have tantrums and they will have a lot of them. It's not your fault. The only thing you can have control over is how you handle it.

9 TIME FOR YOURSELF

Mommy Time

I have an increasingly low tolerance of people saying that raising a child is a full-time job and that there is no time to take for themselves. My mother, bless her soul, worked part-time, kept the house clean, raised my brother and me, and still found time to sit down with a cut of tea and relax. Whoever tells you that it's a full-time job is either trying to get sympathy or wants to scare you out of becoming a parent.

Yes, children are a lot of work. They require a lot of attention and a lot of things change. But take a moment to consider what a baby does. A baby sleeps, cries, eats, and poops. That's it. Young tots don't need you to be a full-time parent. They sleep most of the time. And when they are awake, it's easy to put them in a play-pen wherever you are doing the dishes or washing the floors.

Sure, when a toddler gets a little older, they will require a lot more of your time, but do they take up all your time? The answer is no. And if they do then it is time to sit down and think about what the toddler can do on his or her own.

Children need a lot of sleep. When they are not eating or playing, they are sleeping. Sleeping for extended periods of time. Not all children are that easy, I understand this, but it's important not to fuss over a crying child as soon as they start crying. When they are in their cribs, fed, diaper changed, and obviously exhausted, let them cry it out. It's because they are naughty and know that you give them attention when they are crying. They need to learn that nap-time is mommy time and that is when you get to take the time, make a cup of tea, sit down in your bay window and read a good book.

It might be hard the first week or two. Who am I kidding? It is going to be hard. But after that, you will see that the tot will learn that when you put them in their crib, it's time to sleep because you are not giving in to their demands.

Babies, tots, children, and teens are very demanding, and most parents give in to those demands. You shouldn't because that's why you are not getting the time off you deserve.

Mommy time is essential for any mother, young and old. It gets harder when your family is expanding and you have more than one child running about, but you have to work on a routine to make sure that you get the mommy time.

It's easy to become frustrated and resentful when you constantly live for your children and not for yourself. They need the discipline to know that "it's mommy time." They don't have to be taking a nap. Put them in their playpen next to you while you are watching a movie, even hold them in your arms when they are still small, but you do not have to watch the Lion King on repeat, because they don't understand half of what's going on anyway. Let them play but squeeze your own time in there too.

When you are spending every moment of every day with your kid, it's hard to remember who you actually are. It's easy to forget the person that you were before you had a child and that is so, so very wrong. Children change your responsibilities and teach you many things, but it should never take away the person that you were before you had them. It's not healthy, not for you or your tot.

It's important for a toddler to learn how to be independent from a young age. I remember my mother telling me that her mother used to carry her everywhere, not allow her to play by herself or even get hurt. When she got older, she realized that she was completely dependent on mother. There was nothing she could do without her mom being present.

Sure, the youngling will need help with eating or coloring, but you do not need to hold your hand under the toy at all times to prevent it from falling. They have to go pick it up. This is why so many mothers have this delusion that their kids always need them. They don't. They might be difficult the first couple of days or weeks, but they need to learn that they will not always get what they want just because they are crying. And as such, you will be able to make some mommy time in the process.

Daddy Time

Contrary to popular belief, a father has just as much on his plate as a mother. Sure, he didn't carry the baby for nine months, but he did have to listen to his partner the entire time and when the child is there, the father will get up in the middle of the night to check on the tot as well.

It's not only the mother that is raising the kid and even some fathers don't realize this. Daddy time is just as important as mommy time. When you are at work, it doesn't count as daddy time. You are working, not watching ESPN.

Make sure that you are getting your daddy time along with mommy time. If you two can get it together, even better. Hire a babysitter, get a family member to look after the tot and go out for the night. Make an effort. Your lives didn't stop when you had a child and it never should.

When they are tots, they get difficult, but that is exactly when you need some time to regenerate all that energy for another day with your little bundle of joy.

Don't forget your love life!

Many flames extinguish as soon as you have a baby and it's hard to rekindle what was lost. You must make sure to keep that flame going. Put your kid to bed and cook something nice for your significant other.

Partner time is just as important as me time. A kid shouldn't get in the way of that. Sure, you will not be able to party like you used to, but it doesn't mean there can't be a flame at all. Whether it's in the bedroom, at a restaurant, or in front of the TV with the toddler playing at your feet, don't let it die out. Just because the toddler is around doesn't mean you have to pay attention to them. They know that you are there, and they know that they are safe. Watch your movie in peace

CONCLUSION

I have spent many hours deliberating on how I should end this book. Instead of going the traditional route of "what have we learned" or "the moral of the story," I am ending this with a story. Yes, another story. This is a good one though, I promise.

It was in September when we got the call that my little nephew was born. Oh, he was an ugly baby, but aren't all of them? He looked exactly like my brother when he was born and had my sister-in-law's beady little eyes.

I didn't lie to my brother and tell him that he was beautiful. In fact, my brother pulled me to one side and told that he thinks his wife had an affair with an alien because the child was not as pretty as those Instagram kids. I laughed and told him this was probably exactly what our father said when he was born. I was a beautiful baby, so I had the right to say this. He's my brother, after all.

Afterward, each one of us had a chance to hold the little person. I made a promise to him that day. When I was holding him, I knew how many problems this kid was going to give us. If he was anything like his father, I knew that my brother would call us in the middle of the night in a panic because the kid is missing only to find him in the treehouse munching away on chocolate bunnies.

They announced that my partner and I would be godparents, my sister-in-law too out of it to have a say in it, and I felt my heart swell for the kid on the spot.

I didn't know that this meant I was going to be their designated babysitter. Now that I think about it, it seems more and more apparent they only did it for free babysitting. It didn't matter though. The child crawled his way into my heart from the first moment I saw those beady eyes.

Now he's a toddler and believe you me, the child is busy. I found him climbing my fridge once. I told my brother it's because of all the superhero movies but he had none of it.

So, one day, my brother and I were sitting on the back porch, watching over the little man running around and falling on his face because he doesn't have the proper balance yet. He refuses to cry though and gets angry when anyone tries to help him.

So, there we are sitting, watching the kid fall and fall again. That's when my brother turns to me and says the one thing that I never expected him to say: "if it wasn't for you, I don't think he would have turned into the kid he is now."

Confused, I asked him what he meant, and he replied with this was "don't think I don't know it's you that put that toddler discipline guide in his diaper bag. Yeah, wipe that grin off your face. At first, the wife was furious because 'do these people think we can't raise a child?' It was an all-out war. So, I told her that 'they probably do because we are raising a demon spawn.' You don't know the half of what he was doing. We couldn't leave him alone for a second. It was only when he was with you that he seemed to calm down a bit." Emphasis on "a bit."

I didn't tell him that, though, I just listened. He continued "I always thought yelling was going to help but then I read the stuff in your book and I realized that I was doing it all wrong all this time. Mom and dad hardly ever yelled at us, do you remember? They'd just guilt us into apologizing or doing things that we refused to do otherwise."

"So, the kid is better now?" I asked and my brother chuckled.

"Despite what the wife might tell you, yes. Yes, he is. Look at him. A month ago, he would've pulled out every flower from the garden by now. Now he's just a child." There was a smile on his face then. One that made me smile as well.

I never meant to publish a book on toddler discipline. I merely did it to help my brother and his wife. She's come around too, I think. Perhaps she realized that doing nothing was a lazy man's solution. There's a difference between disciplining your child with smacks and yelling and disciplining them the smart way. The way that won't leave lingering regrets on your part or on your child's.

A child needs discipline, always has, always will. I hope that this book will help a lot of other parents realize that too. And I hope that it will make the lives of kids and parents alike, much, much easier.

I don't claim to know everything, but I know what works. I don't believe in advanced reverse psychology, yelling like a madman, or smacking the kid so they can't sit for a week. I believe in discipline the smart way. The way that needs the least amount of effort and leaves the least amount of mental scars and damage.

Yelling leaves mental scars that might never heal. When someone yells, they are bound to be insulting and that's exactly what we don't want to do to our children. Nothing makes me angrier than parents degrading their children. It makes my blood boil.

The fact of the matter is there is something that works for everyone and the tips in this book is a mixture of everything I have learned over the years with my own children and others'. These things work. If my brother's demon spawn was able to calm down enough to smell the flowers instead of stomping on them, then it's worth a shot for everyone else.

May this book help other people as much as it helped my brother. Happy parenting!

www.ingramcontent.com/pod-product-compliance
Lightning Source LLC
Chambersburg PA
CBHW071255070526
44583CB00017B/2486